D1243491

TRAIL OF TEARS

Lynn Peppas

CRABTREE
Publishing Company
www.crabtreebooks.com

Crabtree Publishing Company
www.crabtreebooks.com

Author: Lynn Peppas
Publishing plan research
   and development: Reagan Miller
Editors: Rachel Minay, Kathy Middleton
Proofreader: Kelly McNiven
Photo Researchers: Rachel Minay, Lynn Peppas
Design: Tim Mayer
Cover design: Ken Wright
Production coordinator and
   prepress tecnician: Ken Wright
Print coordinator: Margaret Amy Salter

Produced for Crabtree Publishing
Company by White-Thomson Publishing

Photographs:
Alamy: North Wind Picture Archives: pp.
14–15, 19; William S. Kuta: pp. 44–45; Corbis:
National Geographic Society: pp. 1, 36–37;
Library of Congress: pp. 10–11, 12–13, 20,
21, 33; Max D. Standley: "Arrival in Indian
Territory (Trail of Tears)", Max D. Standley,
courtesy of R. Michelson Galleries www.
RMichelson.com: pp. 40–41; "Forced Move
(Trail of Tears)", Max D. Standley, courtesy
of R. Michelson Galleries www.RMichelson.
com: pp. 34–35; "The Trail of Tears", Max D.
Standley, courtesy of R. Michelson Galleries
www.RMichelson.com: front cover, pp. 38–39;
Shutterstock: CLM: p. 3; optimarc: p. 18;
Sarah Cates: p. 43; SuperStock: Newberry
Library: pp. 25, 28, 26–27; Science and Society:
pp. 8–9; Topfoto: The Granger Collection:
pp. 4–5, 6–7, 22–23, 30–31, 32–33; Wikimedia:
pp. 16–17, 24, 29, 42.

Library and Archives Canada Cataloguing in Publication

Peppas, Lynn, author
   Trail of Tears / Lynn Peppas.

(Crabtree chrome)
Includes index.
Issued in print and electronic formats.
ISBN 978-0-7787-1174-2 (bound).--ISBN 978-0-7787-1187-2 (pbk.).--
ISBN 978-1-4271-1364-1 (pdf).--ISBN 978-1-4271-8927-1 (html)

   1. Trail of Tears, 1838-1839--Juvenile literature. 2. Cherokee
Indians--Relocation--Juvenile literature. I. Title. II. Series:
Crabtree chrome

E99.C5P38 2013   j973'.04975   C2013-906228-9
                                             C2013-906229-7

Library of Congress Cataloging-in-Publication Data

Peppas, Lynn.
   Trail of tears / Lynn Peppas.
      pages cm. -- (Crabtree chrome)
   Includes index.
   ISBN 978-0-7787-1174-2 (reinforced library binding : alk.
paper) -- ISBN 978-0-7787-1187-2 (pbk. : alk. paper) -- ISBN
978-1-4271-1364-1 (electronic pdf : alk. paper) -- ISBN 978-1-
4271-8927-1 (electronic html : alk. paper)
   1. Trail of Tears, 1838-1839. 2. Cherokee Indians--
Relocation. 3. Cherokee Indians--Government relations. 4.
Cherokee Indians--History--19th century. I. Title.

   E99.C5P387 2014
   975.004'97557--dc23
                                        2013036064

Crabtree Publishing Company
www.crabtreebooks.com   1-800-387-7650

Printed in Canada/102013/BF20130920

Published in Canada
Crabtree Publishing
616 Welland Ave.
St. Catharines, ON
L2M 5V6

Published in the United States
Crabtree Publishing
PMB 59051
350 Fifth Avenue, 59th Floor
New York, New York 10118

Published in the United Kingdom
Crabtree Publishing
Maritime House
Basin Road North, Hove
BN41 1WR

Published in Australia
Crabtree Publishing
3 Charles Street
Coburg North
VIC 3058

Contents

Native Peoples

Remembering the Past

This is how one survivor from the Trail of Tears described it: "Long time we travel on way to new land. People feel bad when they leave old nation. Women cry and make sad wails. Children cry and many men cry, and all look sad like when friends die, but they say nothing and just put heads down and keep on go towards West. Many days pass and people die very much. We bury close by Trail." (From the *Daily Oklahoman*, April 7, 1929)

Trail of Tears

The Trail of Tears describes a period in American history when many Native people were removed by force from their homes in the eastern part of the United States. Made to march hundreds of miles to a new Indian Territory, they suffered from disease, starvation, and cruelty at the hands of some of the government soldiers. At the end of his peoples' journey west, a Choctaw chief told a newspaper reporter that the journey had been "a trail of tears and death."

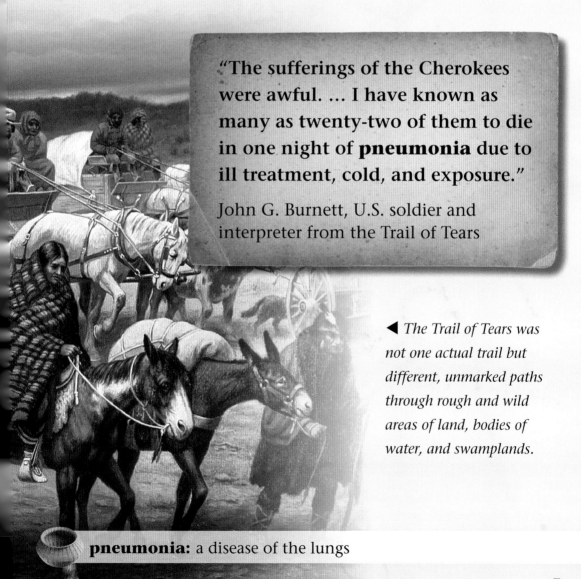

"The sufferings of the Cherokees were awful. ... I have known as many as twenty-two of them to die in one night of **pneumonia** due to ill treatment, cold, and exposure."

John G. Burnett, U.S. soldier and interpreter from the Trail of Tears

◀ *The Trail of Tears was not one actual trail but different, unmarked paths through rough and wild areas of land, bodies of water, and swamplands.*

pneumonia: a disease of the lungs

First in North America

Native people were the first people to settle the land in what is now known as North America. They have lived here for over 10,000 years. A native is a person whose **ancestors** are from the same area that he or she was born in. By the 1500s, millions of Native people from thousands of different groups, called nations or tribes, lived across North America.

In Harmony with Nature

Different nations spoke different languages and had different customs. However, many tribes shared some of the same beliefs. Most had a great respect for nature and the land. They believed that plants and animals had special powers. Native people only killed the animals they needed to survive and used all the parts of those they did kill. They ate all the meat and used skins for clothing. They used bones and antlers for tools.

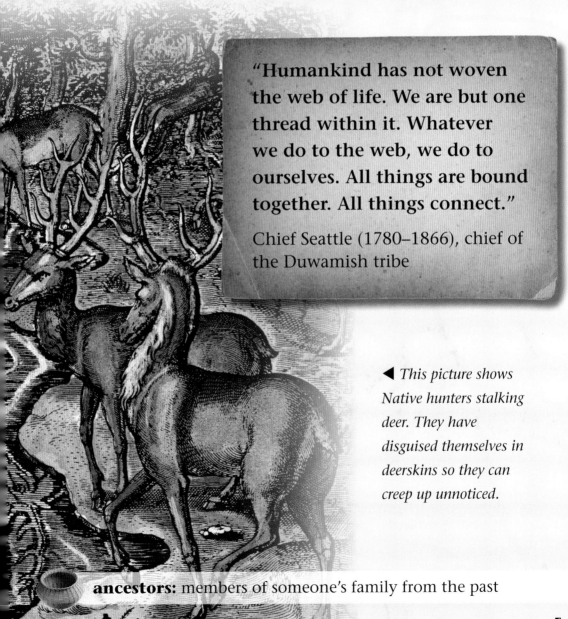

"Humankind has not woven the web of life. We are but one thread within it. Whatever we do to the web, we do to ourselves. All things are bound together. All things connect."

Chief Seattle (1780–1866), chief of the Duwamish tribe

◀ *This picture shows Native hunters stalking deer. They have disguised themselves in deerskins so they can creep up unnoticed.*

ancestors: members of someone's family from the past

Nations of the Southeast

East of the Mississippi River, the southeast region of North America has areas of dense forests, hills and mountains, swamps, and coastal plains. This region was home to the Choctaw, Cherokee, Seminole, Chickasaw, and Creek tribes, as well as others. Although each nation had their own language, and separate customs, most were farmers who chose to settle in an area. They grew crops, such as maize, beans, and squash, hunted animals, fished, and gathered berries, nuts, and wild plants for food and medicines.

▼ *People of the Southeast Woodlands settled in an area and built homes rather than moving from place to place. This picture shows a Creek house in 1791.*

War and Peace

Some Native nations of the southeast were warlike, such as the Creek and Cherokee nations. Sometimes tribes fought against other tribes or against European settlers for land. Some tribes fought **civil wars** against each other, such as the Creek War (1813–14). Some Native nations sided with either the French or British forces and fought against enemy Europeans and their allied Native forces in wars such as the French and Indian War (1754–63) and the War of 1812. The Choctaw were a peaceful nation.

People of the Cherokee nation believed that they lived at the center of Earth. To them, the east meant success, west meant death, north was trouble and defeat, and south was peace and happiness.

civil wars: wars fought between people from the same country

Deadly Introduction

The Arrival of Europeans

By the 1600s, European countries, mainly France, England, and Spain, had claimed land and set up **colonies** on the east coast of America. By 1790, almost 4 million European settlers had moved to the region onto lands that Native people had always lived freely on.

Changing How They Lived

The Native people's way of life changed dramatically with the arrival of these new settlers. The Europeans introduced new animals, such as horses, new plants, and new farming methods to Native farmers. They spread the religion of Christianity among the tribes. Settlers also brought with them new weapons. The gun soon replaced the traditional bow and arrow. Diseases such as flu, smallpox, and measles were also spread to the Native people, who had no immunity, or natural resistance, to them. Illness wiped out entire tribes.

European settlers knew how deadly diseases such as smallpox were to the Native people. Some settlers gave them blankets infected with smallpox, trying to spread the disease.

◄ *Native people did not know, early on, that they might catch deadly diseases from the newly arrived European settlers.*

colonies: areas under the control of another country

Settlers and the Land

Tensions built up between the two groups over rights to the land. Native people believed that land was shared between the community or tribe. But the U.S. government and settlers had very different ideas about who owned the land. Land that Native people once lived on was sold by the government and privately owned by the white settlers.

Spreading Fear

Most settlers feared Native people, although many had never actually met any. This is what the American government and business leaders wanted. They spread stories in newspapers and poster advertisements portraying Native people as violent and inhuman. In this way, new settlers would not feel sorry for pushing Native families from their lands to be **relocated** out west.

Famous American author, James Fenimore Cooper, wrote a novel about Native people called *The Last of the Mohicans* in 1826. The story has been made into movies, television shows, a stage play, three comic books, and an opera.

This movie poster is from a later time period but shows a typical image of how Native people were portrayed as savage and a threat to settlers.

relocated: moved to another place

13

Manifest Destiny

By the end of the 1700s, almost 4 million people had come from Europe to settle on the east coast of North America. The U.S. government and settlers believed in "manifest destiny"—the belief that the United States should expand throughout all of North America. But they also believed that Native people got in the way of this destiny, or rightful goal.

Squatters

A squatter is a person who settles on land that is owned by someone else without permission or payment. Some settlers moved into territory owned by Native tribes and settled on their land. Sometimes Native people attacked squatters to get them to leave. The settlers complained to the U.S. government and asked for protection from attack.

◀ *Some Native tribes forced squatters from their lands. White squatters complained to the U.S. government who usually decided that the Native people should be the ones to move.*

In 1791, the U.S. government and the Cherokee nation signed the **Treaty** of Holston. This established the boundaries of the Cherokee territory, and allowed the Cherokee to punish squatters.

treaty: agreement made in writing between two groups

Assimilation and Removal

Presidential Policies

The American Revolution ended in 1781. The first U.S. president, George Washington, encouraged Native people to **assimilate**—or adopt white ways. The third U.S. president, Thomas Jefferson, argued that Native people would become more "civilized" if they signed treaties and gave up their lands.

Andrew Jackson and the War of 1812

The War of 1812 was fought between Americans and the British. Some Native tribes joined forces with the British because the British promised to end American expansion to the west. U.S. President Andrew Jackson felt that because some Native people had helped the British forces, their land should be taken from them.

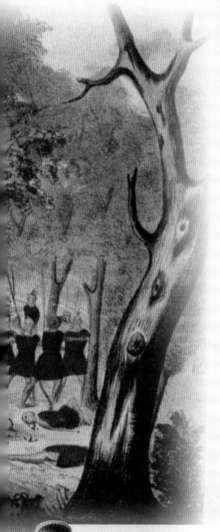

At this time, the U.S. government called the Cherokee, Choctaw, Chickasaw, Creek, and Seminole nations the Five Civilized Tribes. They were called "civilized" because some had adopted the European settlers' way of life by farming and becoming religious.

◀ *Tecumseh was a Native chief who fought against Americans in the War of 1812. He was killed at the Battle of the Thames.*

assimilate: to become part of another society or culture

Gold Rush

Gold was discovered in the mountains of northern Georgia on Cherokee lands in 1828. Within a year, tens of thousands of white **prospectors** crowded onto Cherokee lands to mine for gold. In 1829, Georgia's state government banned all Cherokee people from mining gold on their own lands, yet allowed the white prospectors to continue.

◄ *Gold rushes such as the one in 1828 brought tens of thousands of hopeful settlers to areas such as Georgia.*

"It seemed within a few days as if the whole world must have heard of [the discovery of gold], for men came from every state I had ever heard of ... acting more like crazy men than anything else."

Benjamin Parks

▶ *Gold prospectors rushed to a small Cherokee town named Talonega in 1828. The town was renamed Dahlonega in 1837. The word Dahlonega means "gold" in Cherokee.*

Georgia Gold Lottery

Tensions between the Cherokee and the white settlers grew even more with the Gold Lottery of 1832. The lottery gave Cherokee lands to white settlers. The Cherokee nation took the matter to the U.S. Supreme Court but lost. Forty-acre (16-hectare) land grants were given to white settlers whose names were drawn in the lottery. Cherokee people were not allowed to take part.

prospectors: people who search for valuable minerals

Land Wanted

Nations such as the Cherokee, Creek, Choctaw, Chickasaw, and Seminole did what the U.S. government wanted them to—they assimilated. They became much like the white settlers. They learned English. Some went so far as to use black slaves to work the land on their farms. But white settlers, especially those in Georgia, wanted Native people's lands to grow their cotton crops on. They squatted on their lands. Some squatters made even more trouble by stealing from—and attacking—Native families.

▼ *The five "civilized" Native nations hoped to live peacefully with European settlers by operating large farms and educating their people. This picture shows Sequoyah, a Cherokee who created a writing system. His system made reading and writing in Cherokee possible for the first time.*

Indian Removal Act of 1830

The state of Georgia pushed to have all Native nations completely removed. President Andrew Jackson signed the Indian Removal Act into law on May 28, 1830. Although the move was supposed to be **voluntary**, Native people and their slaves had no choice but to move from their homeland to Indian Territory (see panel on page 41). Some left voluntarily. Others, such as the Cherokee, fought the decision in court.

▲ *Andrew Jackson and other supporters of the Indian Removal Act argued it would be better for Native people to relocate so squatters would not bother them.*

"[The Cherokee] have a printing press ... have shoes and stockings ... cultivate fields ... I hope this nation will soon become civilized and enlightened."

Sally Reese, a Cherokee girl, writing in 1828

voluntary: done according to a person's own free will

Voluntary Removal

No Native person wanted to leave their land in the east but many saw it as **inevitable**. Some nations, such as the Choctaw and Chickasaw, moved voluntarily. Some Seminole and Creek tribes also moved voluntarily, but most had to be forced. A small group of Cherokee also decided to move west. Voluntary removals were organized by the Native people themselves. They were not accompanied by U.S. soldiers.

> "What is to become of the Indians? Have they any rights? If they have, What are these rights? And how are they to be secured?"
>
> Jeremiah Evarts, a missionary, writing under the pen name William Penn, in 1829

▲ *The Trail of Tears went through land and water. Flatboats were often pulled by steamboats through the Tennessee, Ohio, Mississippi, and Arkansas rivers.*

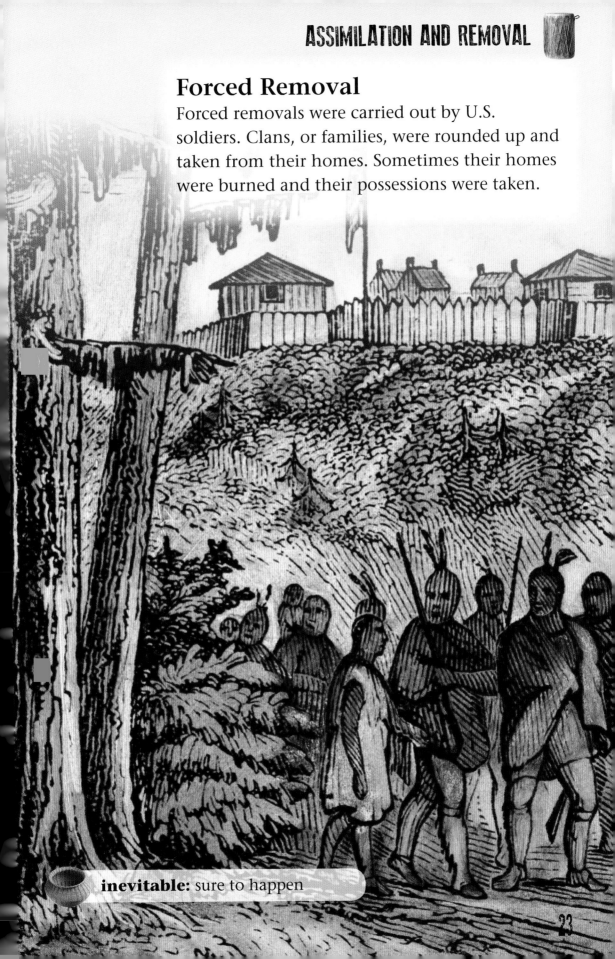

Forced Removal

Forced removals were carried out by U.S. soldiers. Clans, or families, were rounded up and taken from their homes. Sometimes their homes were burned and their possessions were taken.

inevitable: sure to happen

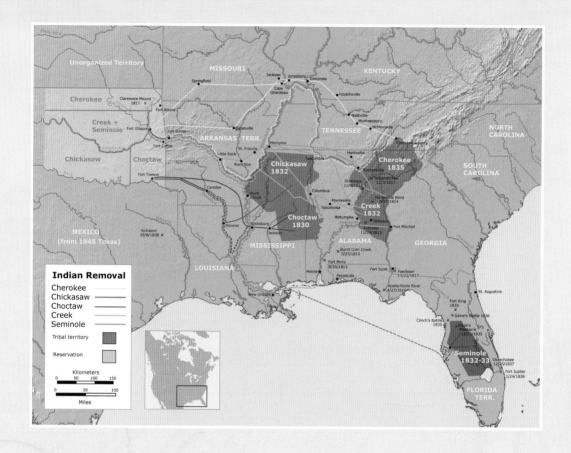

Choctaw Removal

In 1830, Choctaw chiefs signed the Treaty of Dancing Rabbit Creek. They were the first of the nations to voluntarily move to Indian Territory. About 15,000 Choctaw began the 350-mile (563-kilometer) walk in October 1831. Some wealthy Choctaw brought about 6,000 black slaves with them. Most Choctaw were poor and had very little of value to bring with them. Two more removals took place in 1832 and 1833.

▲ *This map shows that the Trail of Tears was not one trail but many. It also shows the vast distances the Native people were made to travel.*

About 2,500 Choctaw and 3,200 Creek tragically lost their lives during their removal on the Trail of Tears.

Creek Removal

The Creek nation signed the Treaty of Cusseta in March 1832. The treaty gave all Creek lands east of the Mississippi River to the U.S. government. In return they were allowed to keep a small area of their land. However, white settlers began squatting or cheating the Creek out of their remaining land. Angry Creek **warriors** attacked settlers during the Second Creek War in 1836. The U.S. military captured the Creek warriors and their families and forced them from their lands. By 1837, over 15,000 Creek people and their slaves were forced to move west.

▶ *Some Native nations, such as the Choctaw, relocated peacefully. Others, such as the Creek (Muscogee), put up a fight before being forced to move. This picture shows a Creek warrior.*

 warriors: experienced soldiers or fighters

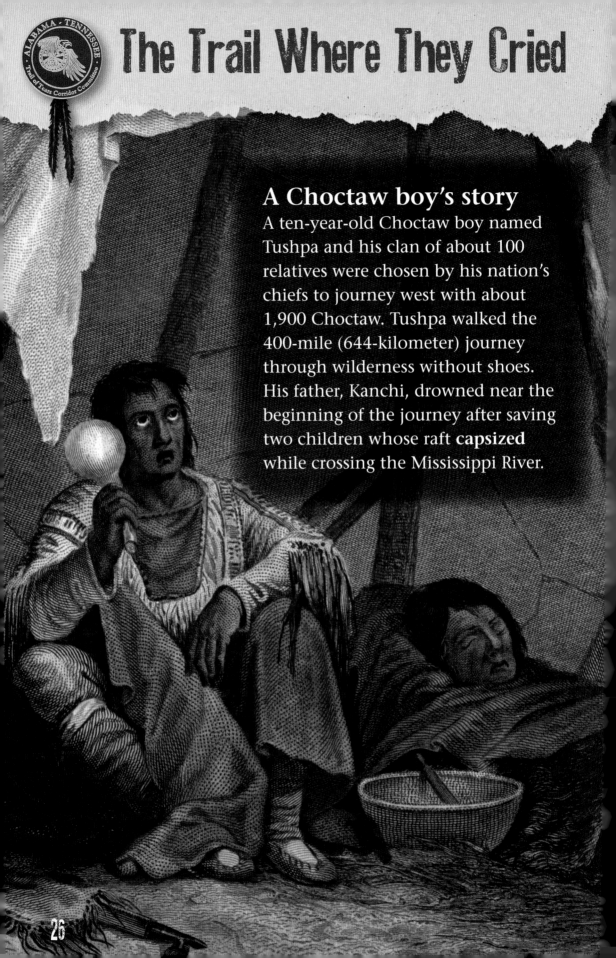

A Choctaw boy's story

A ten-year-old Choctaw boy named Tushpa and his clan of about 100 relatives were chosen by his nation's chiefs to journey west with about 1,900 Choctaw. Tushpa walked the 400-mile (644-kilometer) journey through wilderness without shoes. His father, Kanchi, drowned near the beginning of the journey after saving two children whose raft **capsized** while crossing the Mississippi River.

Tushpa's Trail of Tears

Tushpa and his people waded through mud and water well past their knees for days through swamplands. Many became sick. Near Little Rock, Arkansas, a young boy died of dysentery. The sickness quickly spread and killed others. Even though they had traveled for months, and were only about 50 miles (80 kilometers) away from their new homeland, the Choctaw had to stop to care for those who were sick. Tushpa's mother was one of the many who died. Tushpa eventually arrived at the Indian Territory, but he had lost both his parents on the Trail of Tears.

◄ *Native healers used natural herbs to help cure others. But on the Trail of Tears they did not have herbs to heal others. They did not know how to help.*

"Friends, my attachment to my native land is strong— that cord is now broken; and we must go forth as wanderers in a strange land!"

From a letter written by Choctaw Chief George Hawkins, 1832

capsized: turned over in the water

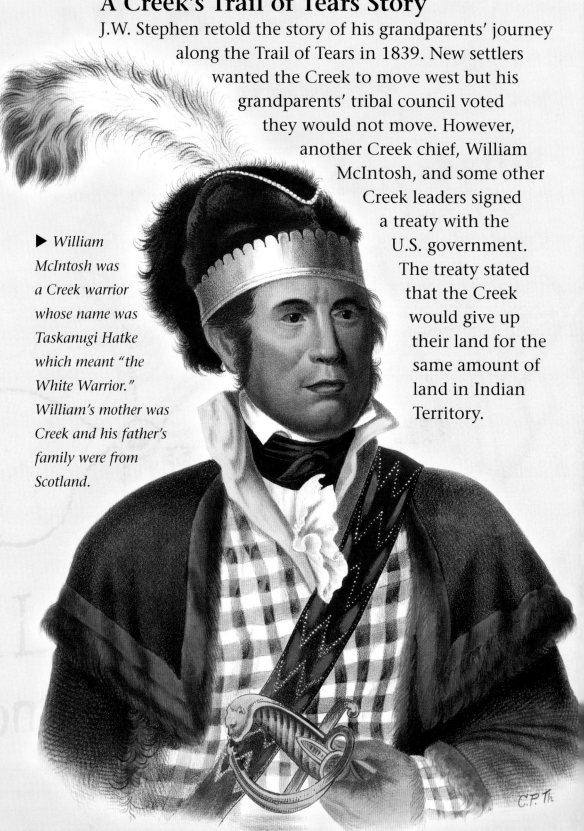

A Creek's Trail of Tears Story

J.W. Stephen retold the story of his grandparents' journey along the Trail of Tears in 1839. New settlers wanted the Creek to move west but his grandparents' tribal council voted they would not move. However, another Creek chief, William McIntosh, and some other Creek leaders signed a treaty with the U.S. government. The treaty stated that the Creek would give up their land for the same amount of land in Indian Territory.

▶ *William McIntosh was a Creek warrior whose name was Taskanugi Hatke which meant "the White Warrior." William's mother was Creek and his father's family were from Scotland.*

▲ *This section of the Trail of Tears survives today. It is in Arkansas and was part of the military road that ran between Memphis and Little Rock. Many Creek, as well as other tribes, traveled this route.*

Treaty and Treason

When others in the tribe heard about the treaty signing they accused William McIntosh of **treason** and killed him. They burned down his home. Others who had signed with McIntosh were killed too. In another treaty, the government promised to help the Creek move, and provide them with food while they built new homes. But they did not. Instead, Stephen's grandfather remembered walking the trail barefoot and said he often left bloody footprints in the snow.

treason: betraying one's own people

Chickasaw Removal

The Chickasaw nation gave up 6 million acres (2.4 million hectares) of their homelands for a $3 million settlement from the U.S. government when they signed the Treaty of Washington in 1834. From 1837, the Chickasaw moved west with their slaves. About 500 died on the Trail of Tears. The U.S. government did not pay the Chickasaw for almost 30 years.

Seminole Removal

After signing the Treaty of Payne's Landing in 1832, some Seminole people relocated to Indian Territory in 1834. Seminole warriors who refused to move attacked nearby plantations and military bases. This began the Second Seminole War in 1836, which lasted for over four years. Some Seminole were given **bribes** to move. Others who were being starved out by the military were left with no choice but to move.

Black slaves escaped white owners by joining Seminole tribes in central Florida in the 1700s. Some became slaves of Seminole leaders and others lived as free people in the tribes.

▼ *Seminole leaders fought U.S. soldiers and settlers in the Seminole Wars.*

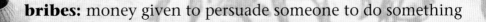

bribes: money given to persuade someone to do something

Treaty of Echota

In December 1835, a small group from the Cherokee Nation council, led by a chief named Major Ridge, signed the Treaty of Echota. The treaty gave the Cherokee land to the U.S. government. But the Cherokee council argued against it because the main chief, John Ross, had not signed it. However, the government **ratified** it anyway.

> "[The Cherokee] may be plundered before our eyes; violence may be committed on our persons; even our lives may be taken away, and there is [no one] to regard our complaints."
>
> Part of a letter written by John Ross in 1836

▶ *This picture shows a Creek chief surrendering to General Andrew Jackson after the Battle of Horseshoe Bend in 1814. John Ross had fought with Jackson and the U.S. military against the Creek in this battle. Years later, President Jackson ignored the help the Cherokee had given him in war and pushed them from their lands by signing the Indian Removal Act.*

John Ross

John Ross was part Cherokee and part Scottish. His ancestry meant both Cherokee and European settlers accepted him. He helped write the Cherokee constitution and became principal chief of the Cherokee council in 1828. Ross gave President Martin Van Buren a petition signed by over 15,000 Cherokee protesting the Treaty of Echota. President Van Buren ignored it and ordered the U.S. military to remove the Cherokee people from their lands.

▲ *Eastern Cherokee warriors hunted down Major Ridge and others who had signed the Treaty of New Echota and killed them.*

ratified: approved and made into law

Cherokee Removal

About 2,000 Cherokee people agreed to move with Major Ridge, the chief who had signed the Treaty of Echota, in 1835. The rest—about 15,000—refused to go. In April 1838, Major General Winfield Scott and thousands of U.S. soldiers were ordered to gather and forcibly remove about 14,000 remaining Cherokee people from their homes. Some Cherokee escaped with their families and lived in unsettled mountain areas.

▶ U.S. soldiers forced Native families from their homes. Some soldiers treated the Cherokee meanly and violently.

"During the Civil War I watched as hundreds of men died, including my brother, but none of that compares to what we did to the Cherokee Indians."

A soldier with the Indian Removal force in 1838

Imprisoned

U.S. soldiers built **stockades** to use as prison camps for Native families they had captured for removal. Living conditions at the prison camps were terrible. They were dirty, there was not enough food, clean water, or supplies, and no doctors to care for the sick. Over 1,000 Cherokee died before they even started on the Trail of Tears.

stockades: enclosed areas with walls made of wood

▶ *The Cherokee*
called the Trail of
Tears "the trail
where they cried."

A Sad Journey

The Cherokee people were
heartbroken as they left for
the west. They left everything
behind: farms, homes, sacred
burial grounds, and possessions.
The government gave each family
about $100 to survive on during the
journey and to begin a new home with
when they reached Indian Territory.
During one of the Cherokee removals,
soldiers' **rations** ran out before they arrived.
The soldiers borrowed money from the
Cherokee people, which they never paid back.

Hardship on the Trail

Many struggled, barefoot, for hundreds of miles. Some described being driven by the soldiers as if they were cattle. The trail was a rugged wilderness. Trees had to be cut down with axes so that wagons could get through. Some traveled during the winter and did not have enough clothes to keep them warm. At night they were forced to sleep on the frozen ground.

> "I hate those white soldiers who took us from our home. I hate the soldiers who make us keep walking through the snow and ice toward this new home that none of us ever wanted ..."
>
> Samuel Cloud, aged nine

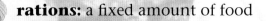 **rations:** a fixed amount of food

Stories of Grief and Loss

Chin Deanawash's husband died as they began their journey on the Trail of Tears. Chin was left to care for three children on her own. Two were too young to walk. She carried one on her back, and the other in her arms. All three of her children died on the way. She had to dig their graves and bury them by the side of the Trail, as many others did with their loved ones, too.

▼ *Native people struggled—many on foot and carrying children—during forced removals on the Trail of Tears. Those who died along the way were buried beside the trail.*

Escape!

One Cherokee man **recalled** how his father, Dun-Ev-Nall Alexander, and some other Cherokee men fought against the soldiers. They took the soldiers' guns, killed them, and escaped to the mountains of North Carolina and Georgia. Other Native people simply ran away while on the Trail. Some were hunted down and killed by soldiers. Others escaped.

> "Or will you, by flight, seek to hide yourselves in mountains and forests, and thus oblige us to hunt you down?"
>
> General Winfield Scott

recalled: remembered a story.

Starting Over

Indian Territory

The Trail of Tears led to an area of U.S. government-owned land west of the Mississippi River. Different areas of Indian Territory were granted to different Native nations according to the treaties they had signed with the U.S. government. Before the Trail of Tears, other Native nations had lived in the area, including the Caddo, Osage, and Quapaw people. Some of these nations moved to other areas such as Texas.

▼ *Native people built new homes and new lives in Indian Territory. But Native lands would soon be reduced again so that white settlers could live on them.*

Cherokee People: East Meets West

The eastern Cherokee people arrived in the west from 1838. Already living on the land were the Cherokee who had voluntarily moved in 1817, and then more recently in 1835. The two sides did not agree on one government for the nation, which sometimes led to violent outbreaks. But by 1859, the Cherokee had built 32 schools and published a weekly newspaper called *The Cherokee Advocate*.

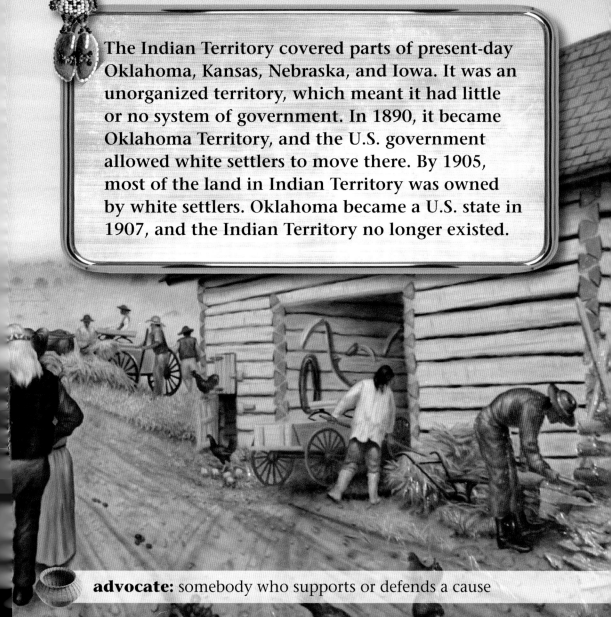

The Indian Territory covered parts of present-day Oklahoma, Kansas, Nebraska, and Iowa. It was an unorganized territory, which meant it had little or no system of government. In 1890, it became Oklahoma Territory, and the U.S. government allowed white settlers to move there. By 1905, most of the land in Indian Territory was owned by white settlers. Oklahoma became a U.S. state in 1907, and the Indian Territory no longer existed.

advocate: somebody who supports or defends a cause

Trail of Tears Today

In 1987, a number of trails traveled by the Cherokee during their removal were named a National Historic Trail. The Trail of Tears historic trails run about 2,200 miles (3,500 kilometers) long. The trails cover water and land routes. Signs mark the path and guide visitors to historical points of interest. Visitors can hike along the actual route that the Cherokee once walked.

▼ *Markers such as this can be found along the Trail of Tears. Each gives a history of Native tribes such as the Cherokee.*

TRAIL OF TEARS

The United States government, unable to conclude an agreement with the duly authorized leaders of the Cherokee Nation, signed a treaty with a minority faction willing to cede the last remaining portion of the original Cherokee homeland on December 29, 1835. Despite the protests of the overwhelming majority of Cherokee people, the fraudulent "Treaty of New Echota" was ratified by the U. S. Senate by only a single vote on May 23, 1836. The Cherokees were given two years from that date to remove to the Indian Territory. When the time had expired only 2,000 of the nearly 17,000 Cherokee remaining in the east had departed their ancestral homeland.

In late May, 1838 General Winfield Scott and 7,000 federal and state troops arrived in the Cherokee Nation to enforce the removal. Cherokee families were forced from comfortable homes into 31 stockades and open military stations scattered throughout the Cherokee Nation in southeast Tennessee, western North Carolina, northwest Georgia and northeast Alabama. From the stockades the Cherokee were sent to the principal emigrating depots near Ross's Landing at Chattanooga, Tennessee, Fort Cass, near Calhoun, Tennessee, and a camp eight miles south of Fort Payne, Alabama.

(Continued on other side)

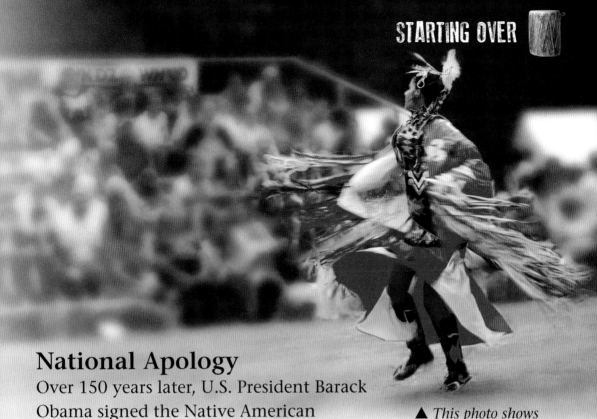

National Apology

Over 150 years later, U.S. President Barack Obama signed the Native American Apology Resolution into law on December 19, 2009. The document apologized for the way the U.S. government treated the Native people. Obama and the U.S. Congress hoped it would help heal bad feelings that still exist today over the unjust treatment of Native peoples throughout history.

▲ *This photo shows a dancer at the annual Trail of Tears Intertribal Pow Wow—a celebration of the culture and traditions of Native peoples.*

"The United States, acting through Congress,... apologizes on behalf of the people of the United States to all Native Peoples for the many instances of violence, **maltreatment**, and neglect inflicted on Native Peoples by citizens of the United States."

From the Native American Apology Resolution

maltreatment: poor treatment

43

Cherokee Nation Today

The Cherokee Nation of Oklahoma is the largest Cherokee tribe in North America. It has over 250,000 members. Many are descendants of the Cherokee people who were forcibly removed from the east. The Cherokee Nation is run by its own tribal government. Schools in Oklahoma teach the Cherokee language and culture to younger generations of children.

▲ *The Cherokee National Youth Choir performs and records CDs of traditional Cherokee songs in the Cherokee language.*

Cherokee Culture: Something to Sing About!

The Cherokee National Youth Choir was founded in 2000 as a way to involve young people in the Cherokee language and culture. Cherokee young people have to **audition** to become part of the choir. It is made up of 40 Cherokee students from grades 6–12 from northeastern Oklahoma communities. They travel to different events across the country.

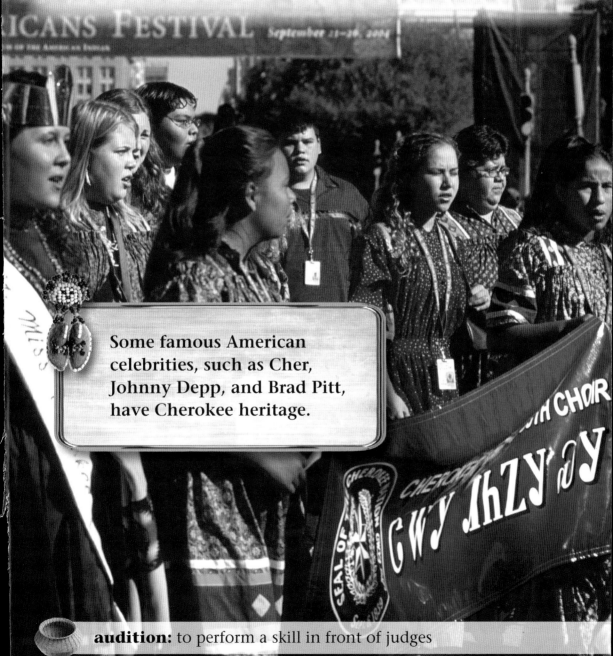

Some famous American celebrities, such as Cher, Johnny Depp, and Brad Pitt, have Cherokee heritage.

audition: to perform a skill in front of judges

Books

The Cherokee Trail of Tears and the Forced March of a People
by John Albert Torres
(Enslow Publishers, Inc., 2006)

The Trail of Tears
by Joseph Bruchac
(Random House Children's Books, 1999)

The Trail of Tears: An American Tragedy
by Tracy Barrett
(Perfection Learning Corp., 2000)

Websites

Trail of Tears—Native Americans for Kids
http://nativeamericans.mrdonn.org/trailoftears.html

Trail of Tears
http://www.cherokee.org/AboutTheNation/History/TrailofTears.aspx

Trail of Tears National Historic Trail
http://www.nps.gov/trte/index.htm

advocate Somebody who supports or defends a cause

ancestors Members of someone's family from the past

assimilate To become part of another society or culture

audition To perform a skill in front of judges

bribes Money given to persuade someone to do something

capsized Turned over in the water

civil wars Wars fought between people from the same country

colonies Areas under the control of another country

inevitable Sure to happen

maltreatment Poor treatment

pneumonia A disease of the lungs

prospectors People who search for valuable minerals

ratified Approved and made into law

rations A fixed amount of food

recalled Remembered a story

relocated Moved to a new place

stockades Enclosed areas with walls made of wood

treason Betraying one's own people

treaty Agreement made in writing between two groups

voluntary Done according to a person's own free will

warriors Experienced soldiers or fighters

Index

Entries in **bold** refer to pictures